SH*T
TOWNS
OF NEW
ZEALAND

THE GREAT KIWI
TIKI TOUR

SH*T
TOWNS
OF NEW
ZEALAND

THE GREAT KIWI

TIKI TOUR

RICK FURPHY AND GEOFF RISSOLE

ALLEN&UNWIN
SYDNEY·MELBOURNE·AUCKLAND·LONDON

CONTENTS

A crucified construction worker on a rural NZ road.

INTRODUCTION

New Zealand is world-famous for its stunning natural scenery — majestic mountains, beautiful beaches and wonderful waterways that we pretend aren't filled with poos. What the country is not renowned for is its regional attractions and small-town events. The Land of the Long White Cloud is not exactly the Land of Disney. In most shit towns of New Zealand you can count the number of genuine attractions on one finger.

Nevertheless, roadside attractions and events do exist in this country — the only caveat is that they are all bizarre, banal or just plain shit. Many of the attractions in this book don't even exist anymore (then again, all the best travel books are out of date the moment you buy them).

For the discerning tourist who is either willing to overlook this shitness or is in fact drawn to it, the attractions, events and other nuggets of knowledge in this volume will fill up any Aotearoa road-trip itinerary faster than Gerry Brownlee's toilet bowl on Boxing Day. Whether you are a supple German backpacker looking for dogging spots or a silver-haired boomer looking for dogging spots, this book will tell you everything you need to know before hitting the road in our mediocre nation.

HEALTH WARNING

THIS STREAM IS POLLUTED

PLEASE DO NOT ENTER

OR USE THE WATER

New Zealand is famous for its clean green environment.

TOP 10

ESSENTIAL NZ ROAD TRIP EXPERIENCES

1. Take a bunch of selfies with 'Big Things'.

2. Spend a relaxing day sitting in a traffic jam.

3. Catch the 'Hamilton flu', aka chlamydia.

4. Pop a tyre on a gravel road in the middle of nowhere.

5. Run over a dozen possums and a couple of pūkeko.

6. Get trapped in your car in the middle of a flock of sheep.

7. Spend half a day queuing to take a photo of an unspoiled wilderness.

8. Get your rental car's wipers and mirrors ripped off by a kea.

9. Get asked if you like New Zealand a thousand times a day.

10. Roll a rented caravan off a narrow winding road.

Bastard.

The Giant Gumboot, Taihape.

NORTH ISLAND

SH1 ROUTE

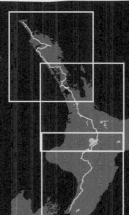

See page 14

See page 17

See page 18

Cape Rēinga Signpost (page 138)

Ninety Mile Beach (page 20)

Hundertwasser Toilets (page 21)

Tāne Mahuta (page 22)

Kumara Box (page 25)

Waiwera Thermal Resort & Spa (page 25)

Muriwai Gannet Colony (page 26)

The Cape Rēinga Signpost.

The Giant Dog, Tirau.

The Royal Easter Show (page 35)

Giant Hypodermic Needle

Footrot Flats Fun Park (page 33)

Queen Street Santa (page 28)

MOTAT (page 32)

Kelly Tarlton's Sea Life Aquarium (page 31)

Infinity Pools (page 136)

Rainbow's End (page 36)

Aotearoa Zoo for Bewildered and Peculiar Animals (page 38)

DEKA Sign (page 138)

Candyland (page 41)

Hamilton Gardens (page 42)

Fieldays (page 39)

Giant Sheep and Dog (page 140)

Giant Poo

Blue Spring (page 136)

Giant Bicycle

Giant Trout

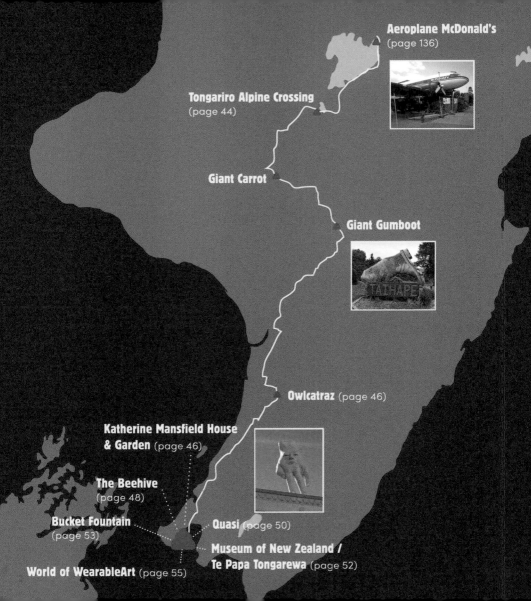

Aeroplane McDonald's (page 136)

Tongariro Alpine Crossing (page 44)

Giant Carrot

Giant Gumboot

Owlcatraz (page 46)

Katherine Mansfield House & Garden (page 46)

The Beehive (page 48)

Bucket Fountain (page 53)

Quasi (page 50)

Museum of New Zealand / Te Papa Tongarewa (page 52)

World of WearableArt (page 55)

The Giant Carrot, Ohakune

Attraction: Ninety Mile Beach

Stretched along the western edge of New Zealand's northern tip, Ninety Mile Beach is New Zealand's most blatant example of false advertising until the '100% Pure New Zealand' campaign. The beach is actually 55 miles long — only 61 per cent of the advertised length — making it a more gratuitous exaggeration than your average Grey Lynn fuccboi's Tinder profile.

It's uncertain where the misnomer originally arose from, but it's suggested it was due to the amount of ground covered by a horse in three days — a horse could reputedly cover 30 miles a day, and since it took three days to traverse the beach it was assumed to be 90 miles long. Unfortunately, this overlooked the fact that the settlers in question owned some seriously lazy horses.

The beach's te reo name is Te Oneroa-a-Tōhē ('The Long Beach of Tōhē'), referring to a highly ranked chief who previously lived in the area — which has the advantage of at least being factual.

Popular activities on Ninety Mile Beach include attempting to toboggan down the Te Paki dunes on a real estate sign, getting your rental car bogged in the surf, and being arrested trying to import 500 kilograms of methamphetamine. Officially a public highway, the beach also featured in an episode of *Top Gear* in which Jeremy Clarkson raced an America's Cup yacht in a Toyota Corolla. Clarkson was later forced to apologise to local iwi for the crimes of disrespecting a sacred site and being Jeremy Clarkson.

Attraction: Hundertwasser Toilets

In general, art is viewed by most New Zealanders with deep suspicion, seen as something created for uncertain purposes by gays or vegans or other people who are almost certainly crap at rugby. New Zealand's most revered artists are Colin McCahon (mostly because he put loads of words in his work so it's almost writing and therefore less suspect) and the budding Banksys who used weed killer to create a penis on Hamilton's Fairfield College field so big it could be seen from space. It's no surprise then that one of New Zealand's favourite works of art happens to be a dunny.

Designed by unspellable Austrian ablutions enthusiast Friedensreich Hundertwasser, Kawakawa's toilets are a garish mess of a building clad in crooked tiles and mismatched colours, with more grass growing in it than a Kaitāia tinny house. The mere thought of it is enough to trigger an epileptic seizure. Initially confused by the premises, Kawakawa residents have grown to love the bogs, their drug-addled brains finding hours of amusement in the trippy shapes and live tree incorporated into the sculpture.

The Hundertwasser Toilets makes the bold claim that it is 'the most photographed toilet in New Zealand', which sounds less like a tourism slogan and more like an award at a sex-pest convention. The claim does ring true, however, as evidenced by the hordes of camera-toting tourists who regularly risk being run over to stand in the middle of State Highway 1 in order to photograph the celebrated shithouse.

Despite being regularly ridiculed and causing numerous traffic accidents, the Hundertwasser Toilets allow lucky Northlanders to enjoy a spot of high culture while snapping off a loaf or copping off with a stranger. If you've ever wanted to drop a deuce in a real work of art, then Kawakawa is the spot for you!

Attraction: Tāne Mahuta

The world's largest living kauri tree, Tāne Mahuta stands an impressive 51 metres (or approximately 102 tacky coffee tables) tall. In typical Pākehā fashion, the ancient kauri was officially 'discovered' in 1924 —

Zealand's second most famous tree celebrity — although the late Pinetree Meads was not an actual tree and clocked in at a somewhat less impressive 1.92 metres tall.

Tāne Mahuta is not just massive — it's also really fucking old, aged somewhere between 1250 and 2500 years, making it the oldest living organism in New Zealand aside from a couple of New Zealand First voters. Unfortunately, the gargantuan tree is now under threat of contracting kauri dieback, a generally fatal disease that is basically the arboreal version of AIDS.

Visitors have been known to be reduced to tears upon visiting Tāne Mahuta — not by the general majesty of the Waipōua Forest but the sinking realisation that they have driven two hours out of their way just to look at a tree.

although local Māori were aware of it the whole time and didn't tell their honky mates in case they chopped it down and turned it into ugly clocks to sell at roadside gift stores.

Tāne Mahuta is Northland's second most beloved tree, after cannabis. It is also New

Attraction: The Kumara Box

Wedged between Te Kōpuru and New Zealand's 'Kūmara Capital' Dargaville, the Kumara Box is an attraction dedicated to one of the world's least stimulating tubers. Run by local kūmara baron Ernie, who does his best job at attempting to make a root vegetable seem riveting, the Kumara Box rates up there with the rest of the world's great vegetable tourist attractions such as Hamburg's Kartoffel-Achteck and Guadalajara's Pirámide de Nabo.

The tour starts with a 42-minute video about the history of kūmara, which is probably 41 minutes longer than the history of kūmara deserves. The Kumara Box also features displays of all the various uses of kūmara through the years, including kūmara dolls, kūmara batteries and even kūmara clogs.

The star of the show is Te Urenui, a prodigiously sized kūmara that has been fashioned into a marital aid of last resort.

The Kumara Box isn't limited to just the wonders of the sweet potato — it also features a surprising collection of inane kitschy tat including a tractor-drawn 'train' made of 44-gallon drums, shitloads of seashells, a wētā cave, and 'New Zealand's smallest church', a tiny shack which resembles less a place of worship and more a consecrated portaloo.

Attraction: Waiwera Thermal Resort & Spa

A popular destination for Auckland's swinging community, Waiwera Thermal Resort & Spa provided multiple distractions for children while their parents indulged in a spot of wife-swapping in the adults-only pool. Another attraction for the key party set was the cinema pool, where they could watch blue movies while engaging in profligate sexual congress.

If stewing in a lukewarm soup of human filth wasn't your idea of a good time, then you could always hurtle headfirst down one of Waiwera's many hydroslides. With names like 'The Twister', 'Speed Slide' and 'The Donkey Punch', these rickety death tubes were assembled in a time before health and safety laws, so they were about as safe as an asbestos sandwich.

Sadly, the complex closed for renovations in 2018 and never reopened, leaving behind a scum-coated concrete wasteland. Without being slurped up and dumped into commercial jizz pits, Waiwera's natural hot springs now bubble up into local backyards instead, boiling people's lawns, gardens and pet cats.

Attraction: Muriwai Gannet Colony

What is a gannet? It's not entirely clear. Is it a 'roided up seagull? Or maybe it's a crackhead albatross? Whatever the case, West Auckland has a metric fuck tonne of the bastards hanging out on a cliff and squawking up a storm. If you are in the mood for staring at a huge mob of munted seabirds, then Muriwai is right up your alley!

Between September and December, the Muriwai Gannet Colony turns into a feathery free-for-all with gannets flocking from all over to have a hoon — essentially becoming that party from *Eyes Wide Shut* but with manky seabirds instead of

Tom Cruise and Nicole Kidman. If watching a bird orgy isn't your thing, then you can return a few months later to witness the products of all the rampant rutting take their first awkward steps into the world.

Like all good sex pests, gannets eventually decide to bugger off to Australia once they have run out of local talent, only to return when they have ruined their credit or been deported. Once returned to their New Zealand homeland, the dodgy bastards sink back into their old lifestyle of rooting and causing a ruckus, never to return to the Lucky Country.

Did you know? New Zealand's most famous gannet was 'Nigel the Lonely Gannet', who lived with a colony of painted replicas on Mana Island off the Kāpiti Coast, and even spent the last five years of his life courting one particular lump of concrete.

Although Nigel's life story is a heartbreaking tale of loneliness, he at least provided researchers with valuable evidence that gannets are really dumb.

Attraction: Queen Street Santa

Haunting Auckland's main commercial thoroughfare for nearly 60 years, the Queen Street Santa petrified generations of children with its mangled and decidedly unfestive cheer. Looking like a patient who'd escaped from the burns ward of a sex-pest prison by commandeering a Santa suit, the crooked Kringle was named 'the Creepiest Santa in the World' by Cracked.com in 2018.

The Queen Street Santa taught us all that Father Christmas was a burns victim who had his face reassembled by a blind plastic surgeon who had learned his

craft by gluing eyebrows onto fish. Compounding the horror was its moving parts: a 'come here, children' beckoning finger and a 'don't tell your parents' wink. For decades, the Jimmy Saville of giant holiday-themed mascots summoned children to share in the magic of Christmas by getting into the back of his windowless van, contributing to more nightmares than Freddy Krueger and pre-bedtime cheese combined.

Waggling the most infamous bent finger this side of Billy Bowden, this was the creepiest giant hand until Quasi. With a face like a dropped Christmas mince pie and a pair of listless misshapen eyes that looked like they belonged to a denizen of Area 51 rather than the North Pole, the 5-tonne fibreglass pest surveyed his kingdom like a giant Scout master on jamboree.

In the late 1990s and 2000s, the Queen Street Santa received a series of facelifts which gradually corrected his deformed visage and instead gave him a more conventional human appearance, including removing his moving parts. This new, less terrifying image was slightly undermined by the addition of a pair of demonic reindeer sidekicks that seemed more suitable for Satan than Santa. Aucklanders were not fooled by the makeover, confident in their knowledge that Santa was still a definite diddler.

After six decades atop Farmers Queen Street, then Farmers Manukau, then Whitcoulls Queen Street which then became Farmers Queen Street, the noncy Saint Nick was pulled down and disassembled in 2019. Like many other dodgy Auckland males of a certain age, he has now retired to Wānaka.

Attraction: Kelly Tarlton's Sea Life Aquarium

Part of the holy trinity of ratshit Auckland school trips (alongside MOTAT and the zoo), Kelly Tarlton's Sea Life Aquarium is Aotearoa's foremost fish prison — an aquatic Arkham Asylum housing an array of undersea reprobates ranging from psychotic stingrays to perverted turtles. Built in a disused sewage tank and named after its founder and New Zealand's home-brand Jacques Cousteau, this Pāremoremo under the sea is the country's best attempt at educating a population who normally learn about marine life from a poster in the fish-and-chip shop.

The aquarium's main attraction is an underwater travelator, which is exactly as fun as riding the travelator at the airport only you can put a crick in your neck looking up at bored fish. It's ideal for anyone who wants to see some sea life while pretending to be a piece of luggage.

Kelly Tarlton's also includes an Antarctic exhibit, so visitors can gawk at a flock of confused penguins waddling about in a big fridge. Adventurous visitors can even be dropped into a shark tank — which sounds more like a method of murder concocted by a Bond villain than something any sane person would fork out a small fortune for.

Attraction: MOTAT

Experiencing a stultifying school trip to MOTAT is an Auckland child's perennial rite of passage — pitched as more a punishment than a reward, many a school year was capped with a day spent waddling around the sprawling museum gawping at crusty old cottages and bedraggled items of alleged Kiwiana.

Nobody knows what 'MOTAT' actually stands for, but it's presumably something like 'Munted Old Trains And Trinkets', which gives a pretty good idea of the sort of dusty crap that fills its floors. A popular exhibit is the Tactile Dome, where children are encouraged to wander around a pitch-black environment grabbing at random objects, making it a paedophile's perfect playground. Early alternative names included the Sex Pest Nest and the Glory Hole Bowl.

MOTAT has proven so effective at both boring and frightening New Zealand's children into

obedience that a sequel was launched down the road — MOTAT 2: Electric Shitaloo! The two MOTATs are connected by a shit tram that only goes as far as the zoo next door, which is still more effective than Auckland's bus and train network.

Despite being a punishing day out, MOTAT endures as an important educational tool for Auckland's youth, teaching them all of the things that make our country boring.

Attraction: Footrot Flats Fun Park

Located on Auckland's feral Te Atatū Peninsula, Footrot Flats Fun Park was built to capitalise on the success of the 1980s animated feature *Footrot Flats: The Dog's Tale*, New Zealand's most beloved children's movie since *Meet the Feebles.* Unfortunately, the short-lived theme park was anything but a slice of heaven.

The park featured an array of sad attractions based on the characters from Murray Ball's classic Kiwi comic strip *Footrot Flats* and its cinematic spin-off, including Dog's Dodgems, the 'Ride Cheeky Hobson' ride, and an animatronic Dave Dobbyn and Herbs singing the opening bars of 'Slice of Heaven' on an infinite loop. Despite it having nothing to do with the park's theme, much of the space was taken up by 'Driver's Town', where young visitors could experience all the thrills of being trapped in Auckland's rush-hour traffic in miniature before being issued with a counterfeit driver's license.

Like any good theme park,

Footrot Flats Fun Park also had the obligatory gift shops hawking a range of overpriced merchandise and charged punters to have their photos taken with depressed students stuffed into sweaty costumes, including a derelict 'Horse the Cat' mascot that looked more like an infernal demon with some pubes glued to its snout, and for some reason, Darth Vader. Footrot Flats Fun Park was so shit that it was basically free advertising for Rainbow's End.

After half a decade of teaching Auckland kids that even roller coasters can be boring, Footrot Flats Fun Park closed down and was replaced by houses. Basing an amusement park on a successful New Zealand film was an idea before its time — it would take Ōtara's Once Were Warriors Waterpark (complete with 'Uncle Fucking Bully' Hydroslide and

'Cook the Man Some Eggs' Lazy River) to prove the concept a winner.

Event: The Royal Easter Show

Every year, Aucklanders celebrate the murder and subsequent resurrection of our Lord and Saviour Jesus Christ by consuming copious quantities of candy floss, watching a burly chap chop down a telephone pole and patting a llama, in a ridiculous ritual known as the Royal Easter Show. Despite the name, the only connection this event has to the royal family is that most of the people running the concessions seem to be inbred. Hosted at the palatial Epsom Showgrounds, the Royal Easter Show features a staggering array of terrible attractions that are only mildly interesting because they are all jammed into the same venue.

The livestock shows are the only time in the year when Aucklanders actually want to look at a cow — the rest of the time they are too busy blaming them for climate change and poo-shaming farmers about unswimmable streams that most JAFAs couldn't find on a map. The Easter Show also provides most Aucklanders' only opportunity to see a donkey up close and personal without ending up on charges — remember, it's only animal abuse if it's done by someone in a Swanndri. Another popular attraction is the timbersports competition, the only time Aucklanders will pay good money to watch brawny men work with their hands aside from certain specialty bars on K Road.

The Easter Show's sideshows are a decrepit collection of

amusements run by a gang of recently paroled sex offenders, designed solely to guilt parents into parting with their hard-earned money to placate their squalling kids for long enough to pay $10 to stick a grimy ping-pong ball into a clown's mouth. The Tilt-a-Whirl looks like something from a documentary about sideshow catastrophes. The Ghost Train has played host to more sexual assaults than Neverland. If you want to get bilked out of $50 while trying to win a $5 teddy bear at a crooked shooting gallery, then the Easter Show is for you!

Attraction: Rainbow's End

In folklore, the end of the rainbow is where you can find a pot of gold — unfortunately, at the end of this particular rainbow you will only find a bucket of barf.

Rainbow's End is New Zealand's best attempt at a local version of the famous overseas amusement parks, but what was intended as a Warehouse Disneyland comes across more like a $2-shop Dreamworld.

Although it was founded by a family of leprechauns (hence the name), none of Rainbow's End's rides appear to reflect that theme. Consisting largely of massive machines that spin you, drop you or jerk you around, the actual theme appears to be '101 ways to make you vomit', making it a great place to visit for thrill-seeking bulimics.

The most popular activity is queuing in long lines for underwhelming rides that finish faster than a fifth-former at an afterball. Other popular attractions include Cinema 180, a geodesic dome that looks more like a secret Scientology

facility than an amusement park ride, and the Bowel Motion Master, a 4D ride through David Lange's colon. The iconic Pirate Ship ride was shuttered after complaints from the Proactive International Sailors' Society (PISS) who claimed that it promoted stereotypes about their community and contributed to ongoing prejudice against eyepatch-wearing sea-dwellers.

Located in the heart of South Auckland, Rainbow's End also includes rides that reflect the local culture: hot-wired dodgems, the 'Rob-a-Dairy-Go-Round', and the world's only roller-coaster with a view of a district court. Lucky kids who have their birthday party at Rainbow's End can learn how to cook meth from a cartoon dinosaur and get jumped into the Crips while playing pass-the-parcel.

The most exciting thing that has ever happened at Rainbow's End was when the Log Flume was set alight by arsonists and patrons were able to enjoy the sight of animatronic frogs melting while being overwhelmed by toxic fumes.

Attraction: Aotearoa Zoo for Bewildered and Peculiar Animals

Located in Franklin, Aotearoa Zoo for Bewildered and Peculiar Animals (formerly the Meremere Institute for Low Functioning Defective Terrestrial Fauna, or MILFDTF) houses an impressive array of creatures that have been rehomed from defunct circuses and botched laboratory experiments. Exhibits include a depressed miniature pony, a bipolar bear, and a perpetually masturbating monkey named Sprinkles.

One of the zoo's most popular sections is the Island of Interspecies Amore, which features animals that have formed cross-breed relationships that defy the natural order and the will of God. This attraction is popular with parents attempting to teach their children that while 'any hole is a goal', all good relationships are built on a strong basis of mutual respect and some serious heavy petting. While such unions can sometimes result in spectacularly novel creatures like ligers and zonkeys, all the Zoo for Bewildered and Peculiar Animals has to show for its crimes against nature is a pig with zebra stripes.

The zoo also acts as a sort of maximum-security prison for animals deemed too dangerous to be allowed to roam the Earth freely but not delicious enough

Sprinkles in action.

to end up in a sandwich. These include a racist wombat, a kleptomaniac llama, a parrot that constantly yells obscenities and graphic sexual threats, and a particularly violent goose with a taste for testicles. Visit at your own risk.

Event: Fieldays

Held at the appropriately named Mystery Creek just outside Hamilton, the only real con-undrum is why anyone would choose to attend. Fieldays is essentially Pride Parade for the Swanndri set — but while the Ponsonby equivalent features burly men in leather having a fabulous time, Fieldays features burly men in Red Bands getting a bit too excited about their awful job.

Popular events at Fieldays include such farming staples as sheepdog trials, tractor pulls and a competitive river-wrecking contest. Another popular fixture at Fieldays is the Rural Bachelor of the Year, where a slew of regional Romeos compete to prove they are the most eligible bloke in gumboots by completing a number of tasks including fencing, quad bike tricks and performing cunnilingus while covered in cow shit.

Mystery Creek is also known for hosting the Parachute Festival from 2004 to 2014, a vehicle for Christian kids to escape the prying eyes of their overbearing parents and experiment with sex, drugs and alcohol while trying to block out the terrible Christian rock 'music' blaring at them from outside their jizz-splattered tents.

Attraction: Candyland

Housed in an abandoned dairy factory in the middle of nowhere and looking like something Scooby-Doo and the gang might investigate due to the presence of a pirate ghost, Candyland disappointed children for decades until its recent inevitable closure. Lured in by scores of billboards promising a veritable wonderland of confectionery, children were suckered into whining their guts out until their parents gave in and pulled over in Gordonton. Generally, parents would acquiesce, because if you were travelling to Hamilton what could actually be worse than Hamilton?

What these defeated families were greeted with was less Willie Wonka's Chocolate Factory and more of a giant pick 'n' mix section staffed by an assortment of disgruntled retirees rather than illegal midget labour. The highlight of a trip to Candyland was watching how boiled candy lollipops were made. At the end of the tour, you could buy an enormous boiled candy lollipop in an array of flavours designed to appeal to the elderly palate — aniseed, lemon, loneliness. These lollipops would enjoy several licks before becoming a sticky abortion that would inevitably end up under the driver's seat until it was retrieved months later covered in fluff and regrets.

Attraction: Hamilton Gardens

A tranquil spot in the heart of the City of the Future, the Hamilton Gardens sit on a former waste-disposal site, following in the Tron's tradition of taking a stinky turd and turning it into a slightly less stinky turd. The star attraction is a series of gardens demonstrating famous international locales, providing all the fun and thrill of visiting a garden in Cairo or the Lake District without the inconvenience of leaving Hamilton.

The Hamilton Gardens are one of the country's premier attractions for the sort of person who gets barred up by a chrysanthemum or a half chub from a daffodil. It's a particularly popular place for local grandmas to take time out from causing car crashes, knitting shit that no one wants and calling talkback radio to complain about interracial marriage, to shuffle around at a glacial pace while poring over plants' private parts.

The Gardens are also a popular spot for newly married Hamilton couples to take their wedding photos, giving observers the opportunity to lay wagers

on how long the marriage will last. For narcotic enthusiasts, it's also the perfect spot to pack a bong and get blazed while contemplating which exotic plants you could shelve and get a reasonable high off.

The Hamilton Gardens are the place-to-be for newlyweds, meth heads and nearly-deads.

Attraction: Tongariro Alpine Crossing

Hiking is for nerds, Germans and prisoners of war. As one of the most popular single-day hikes in the world, the Tongariro Alpine Crossing attracts a steady stream of each. With endless lines of hikers and limited facilities on the route, the Crossing has in recent times become known as much for steaming piles of poo on the path as for its stunning alpine scenery.

The Tongariro Alpine Crossing involves walking across an active volcano — a completely safe activity that has never posed a danger for any tourist ever. If weaving your way through an apocalyptic volcanic landscape sounds like your cup of liquid magma, then book now!

Popular activities on the trail include being scalded by a hot spring, violating cultural prohibitions, and collapsing due to a medical event. If you've ever wanted to be the subject of a search and rescue operation then the Tongariro Alpine Crossing is ideal. Previously known as the Tongariro Crossing, the 'Alpine' bit was added to dissuade tourists from attempting the hike in jandals and rugby shorts after a big night on the turps.

The Tongariro Alpine Crossing takes about eight hours to complete, which is about seven hours and fifty minutes too long.

Attraction: Owlcatraz

A bad joke that somehow became a mediocre tourist attraction, Owlcatraz was New Zealand's pre-eminent maximum-security aviary until its closure in 2020. The sprawling bird prison housed some of the nation's most notorious avian criminals, including Antonie Roni Penguin, Stewart Murray Pigeon, Arthur Allan Tomtit, David Gray Warbler, William Bellbird, Morepork Lundy, and Chatham Islands Black Robin Bain. While the punishing name was enough to elicit groans from all but the daddiest of dads, we're just glad they didn't go with Owlschwitz.

Located in Shannon, Owlcatraz was probably the most popular pun-based animal imprisonment attraction in the Horowhenua — other than perhaps Pigremoremo in Levin or Foxton's Goat-tanamo Bay. It was a great opportunity to see owls up close in their natural environment if an owl's natural environment is a tiny shed.

Much like its San Francisco namesake, there was no escape from Owlcatraz. Unlike its more famous counterpart, attempted escapees from Owlcatraz were usually taxidermied and sold as souvenirs.

If you found owls a little bit too stimulating, there was also a selection of commonly found farm animals such as rabbits, pigs and cows, which made Owlcatraz perfect for people who had recently suffered massive head trauma and needed to reacquaint themselves with what animals are.

Attraction: Katherine Mansfield House & Garden

The birthplace of New Zealand's

KATHERINE MANSFIELD BIRTHPLACE

favourite tuberculosis sufferer and bisexual seducer of cellists, Wellington's Katherine Mansfield House & Garden is a lovingly preserved tribute that also happens to be one of the most boring places on Earth.

Katherine Mansfield is revered as one of New Zealand's most famous creative forces, even though her writing features exactly zero hobbits, vampires or BDSM. Her childhood home is preserved as a museum despite the fact she buggered off to London because she felt that New Zealand was a tedious colonial backwater that was stifling her creativity. Fortunately, the good folks behind the Katherine Mansfield House have maintained the dwelling in period-appropriate levels of stultifying boredom so you can enjoy the exact same levels of mind-numbing monotony that forced its namesake to flee the country.

Mansfield obviously harboured fond memories of 25 Tinakori Road, describing it as a 'dark little cubby hole' and 'a horrid little piggy house'. Interestingly, Mansfield only lived in this house until the age of five, making its historical and literary significance questionable at best. A better tribute would be skipping a visit to her birthplace and instead moving to the south of France.

Attraction: The Beehive

The USA has the White House. The UK has the Palace of Westminster. New Zealand has an upturned yoghurt pottle with a dumb nickname.

Designed by a Scotsman and built by the Ministry of Works, the Beehive is a monument to Kiwi lack of ambition. Resembling something that should be plonked on the forecourt of a dated Te Awamutu motor lodge rather than housing the people who run the country, it seems like the concrete eyesore was designed with the sole purpose of making a building so embarrassing that nobody would ever think to take it over in a coup.

Behind its drab 1970s exterior, the distinctive circular dome is not only tacky but also massively impractical, with many rooms jammed into odd wedges. There's a reason there are very few circular office buildings.

The Beehive has earned iconic status as a daycare for New Zealand's highest-paid beneficiaries, the perfect playpen

for self-important bludgers to spend their days engaging in infantile bickering and achieving serious fuck all at the taxpayer's expense. It even has its own licensed restaurant, where MPs can work on their taxpayer-sponsored drinking problems without the inconvenience of leaving work. If you are lucky, you might see the ghost of Robert Muldoon drunkenly stumbling down a Beehive corridor and declaring a snap election.

Attraction: Quasi

Perennially fingering the roof of the City Gallery Wellington, Quasi is a surreal sculpture of an anthropomorphic human hand in the classic 'two in the pink, one in the stink' pose. As if grafted on in some kind of sick scientific experiment, the hand features a prominent human face permanently fixed in the sort of disapproving sneer commonly found on your average Wellington hipster. Indeed, the loathsome sculpture is almost the perfect embodiment of a Wellingtonian: smug, self-important and ultimately a complete waste of taxpayers' money.

Looming over Civic Square like a deformed superhero, Quasi not only manages to be a truly stomach-churning example of pilfering from the public purse but also poses a substantial earthquake risk — no doubt when Wellington is finally levelled by the inevitable Big One, some hirsute barista will be crushed to death by Quasi's sticky digits.

Strangely, the giant polystyrene and resin pest is not the star of another turgid fantasy epic pumped out by Weta Workshop, but rather an authentic attempt

at another 'iconic' piece of public art like the Bucket Fountain or the Wellywood sign. Like all the most irritating Wellingtonians, Quasi isn't even native to the capital, instead having been imported after his initial home of Christchurch got sick of looking at his terrifying visage.

Attraction: Museum of New Zealand / Te Papa Tongarewa

Known as 'Our Place', Wellington's Te Papa is where New Zealand stores all its old crap. Some bright spark had the brilliant idea of keeping our nation's greatest treasures on reclaimed land at the water's edge next to one of the world's most active faults, so get in now before the whole thing is buried beneath the waves!

Among Te Papa's most popular attractions is legendary racehorse Phar Lap's skeleton, the best chance for children to see what a dead national hero looks like (at least until the opening of the highly anticipated 'Taxidermied All Blacks' exhibit). Another drawcard is the colossal squid — the largest and grossest invertebrate ever discovered in New Zealand (until Gerry Brownlee was elected Member for Ilam). Unfortunately, the expensive upkeep for the desiccated squid corpse has forced Te Papa to cut costs elsewhere by exhibiting underwhelming national icons like vintage kitchen appliances, the Nek Minnit Guy's stolen scooter and Captain Cook's pubes.

Te Papa also doubles as an art gallery, which conveniently allows it to exhibit any old bullshit. In 1998 this included a statuette of the Virgin Mary enshrouded in a condom, which sparked

calls for boycotts, threats of legal action, abuse of Te Papa staff, a physical attack on the exhibit and the assault of a museum guard, in one of the biggest displays of sookiness in New Zealand history.

Attraction: Bucket Fountain

When it was initially erected the Bucket Fountain divided public opinion, with some thinking it was complete rubbish while others thought it was a bunch of bollocks. Now the Bucket Fountain is one of Wellington's most beloved pieces of public art, along with that Len Lye sculpture that bogan broke and that statue of a naked bloke getting his wang out on a wharf.

The Bucket Fountain is a series

of brightly coloured buckets that fill up with water and then tip it into another bucket before spilling water onto passing pedestrians — making it less public art and more public nuisance. Wellingtonians' affection for the Bucket Fountain probably stems from the fact that it's frequently broken, expensive to maintain and utterly ridiculous — in other words, the perfect representation of the capital city. If it had a taste for craft beer and was involved in a polyamorous triad then it might have been elected mayor by now!

An intoxicated Elijah Wood famously urinated in the Bucket Fountain during his time filming *The Lord of the Rings*, leading the water feature to become a site of pilgrimage for Tolkien fans hoping to splash a drop of Frodo's piss on their face.

Event: World of WearableArt

World of WearableArt features a stunning range of costumes slapped together like a primary-school craft project that got wildly out of hand. Most entries can be considered 'art' in the same way as if Michelangelo was asked to decorate the Sistine Chapel ceiling with the contents of a dumpster he found behind a Four Square. The event attracts contestants from over 40 countries (mostly Euro-duds where Kraftwerk is considered music and light bondage is considered a first date).

Popular with females of a certain vintage, World of WearableArt is the sort of twee bollocks that Wellington revels in as New Zealand's home of smug self-importance. While it originally began in Nelson, once the luvvies in the capital got wind of the esoteric nonsense on offer they nicked the festival so it could take its rightful place among other beloved and preposterous Wellington pastimes like craft beer, dub music and national politics.

Given the volume of post-menopausal women swarming to Wellington to ogle a bra made from curdled mayonnaise, 'WoW' also doubles as the busiest date on the calendar for the country's gigolos.

TOP 15

SHIT TOWN SONGS

We've got your Kiwi road-trip soundtrack covered with this playlist of famous songs about New Zealand's shit towns.

1. AC/DC — 'Back in Blackball'

2. The Beatles — 'Strawberry Feildings Forever'

3. The Cure — 'Waikanae Be You?'

4. Dave Dobbyn and Herbs — 'Slice of Methven'

5. Metallica — 'For Whom the Balclutha'

6. Metallica — 'Masterton of Puppets'

7. Metallica — 'Nothing Else Matamata'

8. Queen — 'We Will Roxburgh'

9. Peter, Paul and Mary — 'Bluff the Magic Dragon'

10. Elvis Presley — 'Blue HaWaihi'

11. Elvis Presley — 'Viva Rotovegas'

12. Ja Rule — 'Waihola Holla'

13. Scribe — 'How Many Dudes You Know Rolleston Like This? Not Many, If Any'

14. Simon & Garfunkel — 'Cambridge Over Troubled Water'

15. Frank Sinatra — 'New Plymouth, New Plymouth'

Mega Cow, Morrinsville.

NORTH ISLAND

EAST COAST ROUTE

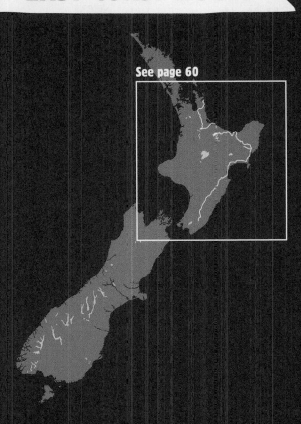

See page 60

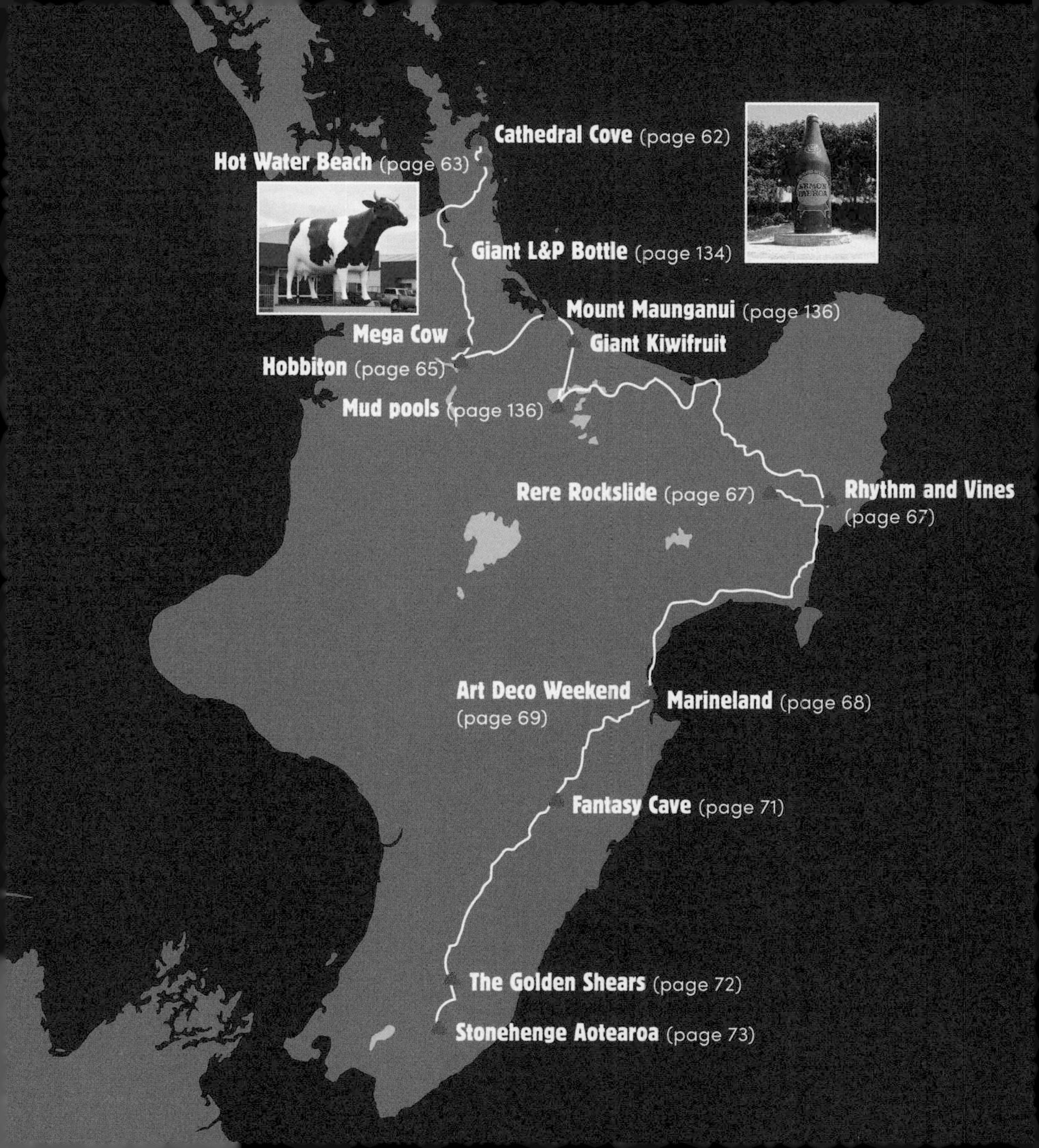

Hot Water Beach (page 63)

Cathedral Cove (page 62)

Giant L&P Bottle (page 134)

Mount Maunganui (page 136)

Giant Kiwifruit

Mega Cow

Hobbiton (page 65)

Mud pools (page 136)

Rere Rockslide (page 67)

Rhythm and Vines (page 67)

Art Deco Weekend (page 69)

Marineland (page 68)

Fantasy Cave (page 71)

The Golden Shears (page 72)

Stonehenge Aotearoa (page 73)

kiwi 360™

The Giant Chinese Gooseberry, Te Puke.

Attraction: Cathedral Cove

Famous for its picture-perfect natural rock archway nestled between two beaches, Coromandel's Cathedral Cove is an iconic (i.e. chronically overcrowded) tourist attraction. Much like a real cathedral, the crowds are worst on weekends. And also much like a real cathedral, half of the people are sex pests just there for a sneaky perv.

Cathedral Cove can be inconveniently accessed via either a punishing kayak marathon or a punishing hour-long hike. The local council has addressed the overcrowding issue by making it even more difficult to get there by banning car parking in the car park, adding another 20 minutes' walking or a bus trip to the already epic slog. It would be easier to get to the Sistine Chapel.

Cathedral Cove served as a filming location for *The Chronicles of Narnia: Prince Caspian*, in which the protagonist children entered the magical world of Narnia through the famous archway. In reality, the most magical thing that can happen to children at the tunnel is magically getting stuck on the wrong side after the tide comes in. The site also featured in a Macklemore music video, in which the woeful white rapper gave a haircut to singer Ray Dalton while wearing a wig to hide his own 'bad guy from *Doug*' operation.

Note: Cathedral Cove is not to be confused with the Cathedral Caves in the Catlins, or the Caved-In Cathedral in Christchurch.

Attraction: Hot Water Beach

Coromandel's imaginatively named Hot Water Beach is, as you might imagine, a beach with hot water. In fact, the name is somewhat of a misnomer — the seawater isn't actually any hotter than at a usual beach, but, due to a geothermal feature, around low tide it is possible to dig a hole and sit in it as it fills with vaguely warm sludge.

Few people have sat on Copacabana and thought 'This is great, but you know what would be better? If I could dig a big hole and sit in lukewarm water the temperature of that cup of tea I forgot about.' Yet Hot Water Beach is inexplicably popular with international and domestic tourists alike, which means on

any given day it'll be jam-packed with half-naked strangers just itching to share your pube-riddled paddling pool.

Hot Water Beach is billed as a 'unique experience', although being nailed to a donkey and flung out of a catapult could also be described as a 'unique experience'. What the brochures don't mention is that you will probably spend the better part of a day digging a hole big enough to bury a camel, but by the time high tide rolls around it will only have filled with enough water to barely reach your ankles. It would actually be bad enough to suggest the whole thing was an elaborate practical joke if the local economy didn't rely on a lucrative spade rental business.

Hot Water Beach is also known for its fierce surf, so if furiously digging a hole with your bare hands like a rodent on P isn't your idea of a good time, then getting sucked out to sea by a deceptively savage rip is also an option.

Attraction: Hobbiton

In the early 2000s, New Zealand surrendered its collective self-esteem to a punishingly long trilogy of films about a homeless bloke assembling a gang of midgets, a fairy and a gnome to go on a really long walk to hiff some stolen jewellery into an angry volcano. For some inexplicable reason, these films became a global phenomenon, and ever since then the country has made a decent living bilking tourists based on the delusion that Aotearoa is actually Middle Earth and that if they visit they might get a tug job from a centaur or something.

A key attraction for Ringholes

is Hobbiton, a crucial set in both *The Lord of the Rings* and *The Hobbit* trilogies, which has the unfortunate situation of being lodged in the Waikato effluent production facility of Matamata. Despite preconceptions, Hobbiton isn't so much an immersive fantasy land as it is a bunch of house façades stuck to some hills in a cow paddock. Featuring all the ambience of your local garden centre, Hobbiton gives touring geeks the chance to hand over a small fortune to gawk at a door leading nowhere.

For its part, the town of Matamata has leaned into its role as the home of Hobbiton, and has now banned any residents above the height of five feet to help preserve the illusion that the whole place is overrun by furry-footed midgets.

Attraction: Rere Rockslide

If you're hankering to hurtle down a slippery slope but require a much higher chance of dying than offered at your local swimming pool, then the Rere Rockslide is for you!

Located 45 minutes outside of Gisborne on the Wharekōpae River, the Rockslide is a 60-metre slimy rock face used by local lunatics and temerarious tourists alike as a water slide. The time-honoured activity involves trepidatiously trotting halfway across the scum-coated rock to the middle of the river, before throwing yourself down the slope on a makeshift vessel like a yoga mat or blow-up bed. It's enough to make your adrenaline, urine and quite possibly blood flow.

If the prospect of careening towards a watery grave on an old tyre doesn't entice you, the Rere Rockslide's other stellar selling point is long-term faecal contamination. Unbeknownst to most of the plebs who dive in like it's the Fountain of Fucking Youth, the popular death trap is usually rated as unsafe for swimming due to copious quantities of cow shit in the river. Considering this unsavoury detail, a more accurate name for the attraction might be the Gisborne Poop Chute, the Tairāwhiti Toilet, the Wharekōpae Wharepaku, the *E. Coli* Coaster, the Diarrhoea Express, the Crap Cannon, the Shit 'n' Slide, the Lazy Colon, the Poonami, the Shartnado, the Shawshank Shit Pipe, or the Hunt for Brown October.

Event: Rhythm and Vines

The East Cape of New Zealand is the first place on New Zealand's mainland to see the light of a new year, making Gisborne the first place to deal with pinga rats. Held every New Year's, the Rhythm and Vines festival sees the coastal city invaded by hordes of Remmers thugs in NBA singlets and bucket hats and Shore girls with bad fake tans. Bringing with them as much beer, cask wine and E as you can pack in a hatchback, and plans to dance, drink, drop, spew, grope and fuck the year away, the R&V crowd are the least welcome visitors in Gisborne since Captain Cook.

Boasting a largely EDM (electronic dance 'music') lineup, the 'Rhythm and Vines' name refers to the fact that the event is held at the Waiohika Estate vineyard (and presumably because 'Gurning in the Grapes' was a bit too on the nose). The festival sells the majority of its tickets before announcing any acts, ensuring that most of the punters are really just fans of getting off their face in a vineyard rather than fans of any of the artists.

Essential experiences at Rhythm and Vines include playing scrumpy hands with half the Grammar First XV, overdosing on dodgy pills that you bought from some dude in Dirty Dogs, and slipping in a puddle of diarrhoea while staggering back to your tent after a SIX60 set.

Attraction: Marineland of New Zealand

New Zealand's pre-eminent marine mammal abuse facility, Napier's Marineland housed dolphins, sea lions, seals and a small handful of other unfortunate animals. It even had a cockatoo, despite the fact that cockatoos have fuck all to do with the ocean. The park was founded in the 1960s when it was considered a bit of a laugh to imprison intelligent creatures and force them to perform mindless tricks for the enjoyment of paying punters.

The number of dolphins that perished over the years is estimated at 80, making Marineland a veritable cetacean concentration camp — an aquatic Auschwitz. To date it is the only New Zealand tourist attraction that is responsible for the deaths of more dolphins than the average Japanese chef/scientist. These included two dolphins that died in 1969 after a couple of hooligans broke into Marineland and fed them nails, an indictment on the intelligence of both the dolphins and the residents of Hawke's Bay.

Marineland was finally shuttered in 2008 when its final inmate Kelly, the dolphin equivalent of Morgan Freeman in *The Shawshank Redemption*, carked it at the ripe old age of 38 after spending several decades in porpoise prison. Marineland is now just a bad memory — or a fond one for dewy-eyed boomers nostalgic for a time when it was considered acceptable to keep a dolphin in a paddling pool despite the fact it was more intelligent than 75 per cent of the paying guests.

Event: Art Deco Weekend

Based in Napier, the self-appointed 'Art Deco Capital of the World', Art Deco Weekend is a two-day-long orgy of kitsch, celebrating the fact that the whole town fell into the sea and was rebuilt in the mawkish style popular at the time. Aimed squarely at people sporting a

stiffy for *The Great Gatsby*, the event attracts scores of visitors (largely Aucklanders, Australians and other undesirables) looking to celebrate 'the good old days' of the Great Depression, World War II and public racism, when women knew to keep their mouths shut and preventable diseases ran rife in places other than Hamilton. It's essentially cosplay for people on Cialis.

Popular activities include taking a ride in a vintage car, patting a dog in fancy dress, or clawing through the rubble to look for survivors. Art Deco Weekend is New Zealand's premier natural disaster celebration (at least until Christchurch's CTV Mardi Gras really kicks off!).

In recent years, the festival has been plagued by hordes of rampant teens celebrating a style of clean simple lines and bas-relief decoration with a traditional Kiwi dose of alcohol poisoning, drunken brawls and public urination.

Attraction: Fantasy Cave

The sort of roadside attraction you'd expect to be run by a family of cannibals, the Fantasy Cave features an impressive array of homemade tat that seems like it was designed to lure victims to a gruesome fate. Despite its name, the Fantasy Cave isn't Dannevirke's premier supplier of marital aids and sexual appliances, but rather a ramshackle interpretation of children's fairy tales and nursery rhymes. The facility features a massive array of incredulous things to delight young and old alike: mermaids, dragons and a functional regional railway service.

The Fantasy Cave has been

compared with other attractions like Rainbow's End and even Disneyland — these comparisons are completely unfavourable, but a comparison is still a comparison! The pinnacle of the Fantasy Cave's event calendar is during December when they roust someone from the AA meeting next door and squeeze them into a Santa Claus costume for the amusement of local tots.

Rumours abound that the Cave is actually part of an alchemical plot to harvest the vitality of children and prolong the owners' already unnaturally lengthy lives. Given some of the walking dead seen around Dannevirke, this theory can't be entirely discounted.

Event: The Golden Shears

The world's pre-eminent farm animal haircut competition, the Golden Shears sees burly rural types flock to Masterton from across the country to find out who can get the most sheep naked in an allotted time period. It's basically Mardi Gras for blokes who wear black Fred Dagg singlets unironically.

The Golden Shears is the biggest event on the Masterton calendar — which says a lot more about Masterton than the Golden Shears. The competition has been described as 'the Wimbledon of shearing', which is technically true in that it's an archaic event that appeals to inbred white people, it requires a huge amount of grass, and some creep from Palmerston North is probably masturbating while watching it.

The Golden Shears plays perfectly into New Zealand's love of sports that we only care about because we win for the reason that basically nobody else knows they exist. Let's be honest: if the Chinese cared about competitive sheep shaving then there is no chance some bloke from Te Kūiti would ever win again.

With shearing not in danger of being added to the Olympics in the near future, the Golden Shears will remain the biggest event on the competitive sheep-bothering calendar, so it's got that going for it at least.

Attraction: Stonehenge Aotearoa

Stonehenge Aotearoa bills itself as a 'unique place', which is a little like saying contracting gonorrhoea is a 'unique experience' — just because there's nothing else like it doesn't mean it's worth doing. It's also a bit hard to claim something is a unique place when it's literally a

copy of somewhere else.

A replica of the famous English landmark, the Carterton Stonehenge is up there with other famous New Zealand replicas such as the Paeroa Eiffel Tower, the Gisborne Statue of Liberty and Hastings Big Ben — i.e. shit.

Stonehenge Aotearoa attempts to replicate the ancient mystery of the original in the decidedly banal location of Carterton with the equally mundane medium of concrete. It's the equivalent of re-creating the Mona Lisa in fingerpaints, hanging it in the toilet and then claiming your bog is the New Zealand version of the Louvre.

Catering to New Zealand's extensive druid community, the bootleg Stonehenge is of particular interest during Summer Solstice events when local druids can be seen reciting prayers, conducting rituals and performing human sacrifices.

TOP 25

SHIT TOWN MOVIES

Get in the Kiwi road-trip spirit with these classic movies about New Zealand's shit towns.

1. *Birds of a Featherston*
2. *Brokeback Mount Maunganui*
3. *Cinderolleston*
4. *Cloudy With a Chance of Blackballs*
5. *Crocodile Duneedin*
6. *Dark Matamata*
7. *Dude, Where's My Kawerau?*
8. *Escape From New Plymouth*
9. *Fantastic Mr Foxton*
10. *Fifty Shades of Greymouth*
11. *GisBorne Identity*
12. *Good Will Huntly*
13. *Haastaway*
14. *John Carterton*
15. *Night of the Levin Dead*
16. *Papatoytoy Story*
17. *The Passion of the Christchurch*
18. *Pokenocchio*
19. *Raging Bulls*
20. *Straight Outta Cromwell*
21. *Stuart Lyttelton*
22. *Taihape Gilmore*
23. *Wild, Wild Westport*
24. *White Fangarei*
25. *Beauty and the Beast of Blenheim*

The Giant Sheep Shagger, Te Kūiti.

NORTH ISLAND

WEST COAST ROUTE

see page 78

The Wind Wand, New Plymouth.

Attraction: Kihikihi Golliwog

The small Waikato hamlet of Kihikihi has little to set it apart from other dairy farming drive-throughs aside from the Kihikihi Golliwog. The great metal minstrel is beloved by the sort of people who revel in being offended by other people being offended, boomers who flap on about 'freedom of speech' except if someone wants to have a crack at the All Blacks or their shit town, and basically anyone who values their childhood memories higher than whether or not they are dehumanising other human beings.

Golliwogs are a particular delight for New Zealanders of a certain vintage who like to complain about 'political correctness gone mad'. The Kihikihi Golliwog provides a pilgrimage point where they can mill about bemoaning the fact that you can't celebrate a racist caricature anymore without being berated by your sooky grandkids. Unfortunately for them, with the exception of Kihikihi's humungous humiliator, golliwogs have been consigned to history like other such anachronisms as the six o'clock swill, smoking on aeroplanes and Winston Peters.

Ironically, Kihikihi is also the location of one of New Zealand's most blatant war crimes, when British forces slaughtered Māori women and children at Rangiaowhia. The site of the massacre is marked with a plaque.

Attraction: Ōtorohanga Kiwi House & Native Bird Park

You can learn a lot about a nation from the icons it chooses for itself. A national bird is

A nocturnal kiwi in its natural habitat.

particularly telling. Australia has the emu. France has the rooster. America has the bald eagle. New Zealand has the kiwi.

As a land of almost exclusively birds, there were many options for an avian icon — the inquisitive kea, the regal kākāpō, or even the fearsome moa. Instead, our national bird is the kiwi, whose defining characteristic is that it is largely terrible at being a bird:

flightless, featherless and with a call that sounds like a guinea pig being hiffed through a wood chipper.

All this would be somehow forgivable if the kiwi were a prolific sight around Aotearoa, but due to the bird's furtive nature and nocturnal habits, most New Zealanders will go their entire lives without seeing one in the wild. The only way to actually witness the national icon is by paying for the privilege of hanging out in a darkened room with a bunch of bewildered tourists to watch the morose bird shuffle back and forth in the gloom and peck at some grubs — something you can do at the Ōtorohanga Kiwi House & Native Bird Park.

As well as being the country's pre-eminent maximum-security prison for our national icon, the Ōtorohanga Kiwi House holds a number of other native birds and reptiles captive, including the tuatara — that ancient, cantankerous bastard of the New Zealand wildlife scene.

Attraction: Waitomo Glowworm Caves

If you have a hankering to descend deep into the bowels of the Earth for the sole purpose of gawking at some glow-in-the-dark maggots stuck to the ceiling, then the Waitomo Caves are the perfect destination. Waitomo means 'watery hole', which is a pretty apt description of the soggy abyss.

Glowworms are only found in New Zealand, which might go some way to explaining why hordes of tourists queue for the pleasure of cramming into a dinghy and drifting through pitch-black darkness. The popularity of the caves has led to them becoming overcrowded with throngs of amateur spelunkers and would-be Sméagols stumbling around the subterranean cesspit just for the brief thrill of seeing a radioactive worm dangling above their heads.

If that isn't enough to put you off a visit, the cave system is also home to a deadly fungus,

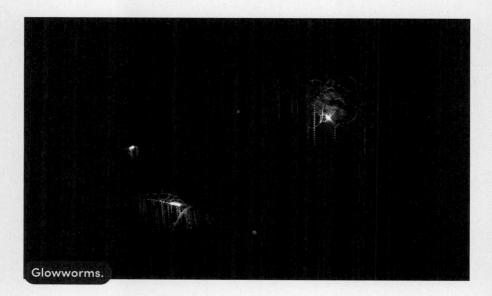

Glowworms.

swarms of albino cave ants, and numerous dryballs tour guides spouting boring science facts and lame dad jokes. Beware!

Attraction: Len Lye Centre & Wind Wand

Looking like a futuristic urinal for giant robots, the Len Lye Centre is the sort of 'art' gallery that you end up with when the residents of New Plymouth (Not Palmerston North, Honestly We're Completely Different) get the idea that they need a bit of culture.

Unlike a proper art museum, the Len Lye Centre doesn't feature ornate paintings of Jesus, incomprehensible modern art scribbles or marble statues with their cocks out, rather focusing on

The world's largest urinal.

'kinetic art' sculptures — basically a fancy way of saying 'a bunch of stuff that goes woosh and looks like room-sized versions of that dongy ball thing your dad used to keep on his desk'.

Like any good creative type, Len Lye actually spent most of his working life nowhere near New Zealand — in fact it's unclear whether he ever even set foot in New Plymouth — but he now finds himself inextricably linked to the Taranaki disappointment. For their part, the Naki nongs have gone all-in on their love for Len Lye, also displaying his 48-metre Wind Wand sculpture under the misapprehension that a fibreglass dong could somehow supersede Mount Taranaki as the city's dominant landmark.

Erected on the waterfront, the Wind Wand is essentially a giant half-flaccid wang that flops around in the prevailing breeze, like a phallic version of an inflatable tube man from a car yard. Locals insist the Wind Wand possesses mystical properties, attributing things such as Lotto wins, impromptu proposals and even the city's massive rate of teen pregnancies to the power of the Wand.

Event: WOMAD

WOMAD stands for 'White Old Mums And Dads' but it actually celebrates world music (or as it's known by most of the world, music), a pseudo-genre only really enjoyed by pretentious honkies as a means of showing how cultured and open-minded they are.

The New Plymouth festival is catnip for hippies wanting to jam out in their house bus to Siamese twins playing an electric banjo, as well as boomers desperate to escape the stress of owning several mortgage-free investment properties by cutting loose to a third-world asylum-seeker playing the butt flute. It's basically Splore without pingas for the parents of the people face-down in their own sick at Rhythm and Vines.

Co-founded by the guy from Genesis who isn't Phil Collins, WOMAD was designed to allow white people racked with liberal guilt to acquaint themselves with other cultures in the most non-threatening way possible. Typical highlights include Mongolian throat singers, Zimbabwean thumb pianists, and the homeless dude who hangs out by the train station playing drums on an empty bucket. New Plymouth also showcases its own culture by supplying a steady stream of intoxicated teens to liven up proceedings.

Attraction: Goblin Forest

Nestled on the slopes of one of the world's most symmetrical volcanoes, Mount Taranaki, the so-called 'Goblin Forest' is surprisingly one of the few distinctive local landscapes that has yet to be used as the backdrop for a CGI-laden adaptation of a beloved children's book.

Despite the name, there are no guarantees you will see an actual goblin — in fact, goblin sightings are about as rare as an Australian with a well-developed sense of shame. However, a detour to a nearby shit town such as Stratford or Hāwera will provide ample examples of the next closest thing.

Hanging mosses, liverworts and ferns make the Goblin Forest look more like Dagobah than Taranaki, but unfortunately, instead of a wise Jedi master the only people you are likely to encounter are fellow tourists and middle-aged Germans with a propensity for dogging.

The Goblin Forest is set to break its cinematic cherry and play a pivotal role in the upcoming adaptation of *Rooty Turnbuckle and the Riddle of the Bi-Curious Centaur*, so visit it now before it is inundated by adults desperate to relive their childhoods in order to dispel the soul-destroying ennui of adulthood.

Attraction: The Ronald Hugh Morrieson KFC

Most places honour their

literary heroes with an appropriate tribute. London has Shakespeare's Globe Theatre. California celebrates the work of John Steinbeck with the National Steinbeck Center. Hāwera has a KFC.

Ronald Hugh Morrieson, perhaps New Zealand's pre-eminent chronicler of the absurd underbelly of small-town Aotearoa, lived a life of relative obscurity despite his impressive literary output. He famously remarked to fellow novelist Maurice Shadbolt: 'I hope I'm not another one of those poor buggers who gets discovered when they're dead', only to die in obscurity in his humble hometown of Hāwera.

Morrieson's novels later served as the basis for classic Kiwi films *The Scarecrow* and *Came a Hot Friday*. Following his death, efforts were made to preserve his residence as a site of literary significance, but the town's fried chicken aficionados won out over book lovers and the house was bowled to make way for a KFC. It is now possible to pay tribute to RHM with a three-piece quarter-pack. Considering his first name, they could have at least made it a Macca's!

Local rumour suggests that Morrieson haunts the KFC's deep-fryer and on quiet nights you can hear lines from *Came a Hot Friday* . . .

TOP 10

LOCAL SEX ACTS

1. The Huntly Handshake
2. The Clevedon Steamer
3. The Waihola Bowler
4. The Gisborne Jizz Bin
5. The Pōkeno Poke
6. The Creampaekākāriki
7. The Peka Peka Pecker Pecker
8. The Queenstown Queef
9. The Wānaka Wank
10. Milford Sounding

The Giant Trout, Gore.

SOUTH ISLAND

EAST COAST ROUTE

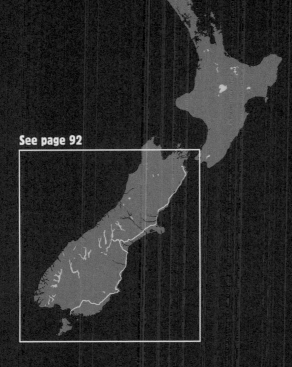

See page 92

MILFest (page 94)

Giant Donut
Pāua House (page 95)

Giant Salmon

Bread & Circus
— World Buskers
Festival (page 96)

Lake Tekapo (page 138)

Steampunk NZ Festival (page 98)

Moeraki Boulders (page 100)

MOSGIEL

Baldwin Street (page 101)

Hyde Street Party (page 103)

Mosgiel Sign (page 138)

Bainageddon (page 104)

Larnach Castle (page 106)

Giant Trout

GORE

Bluff Signpost (page 138)

The new, fire-proof Giant Donut in Springfield,
erected after the original was burnt down by locals.

Event: MILFest

Featuring more moist moot than you can shake a Viagra-fuelled stiffy at, Blenheim's MILFest is New Zealand's annual gathering of women of 'a certain age' and their throng of admirers. Every second Saturday in February, 'Beavertown' is inundated with an avalanche of 'yummy mummies' searching for someone who was still in kindergarten when they lost their virginity to peel off their Lululemon layers and fuck their divorce away. Powered by a literal tsunami of sauvignon blanc, attendees hunt young foreign fruit-pickers and local high-school grads like starving lions — or more appropriately, cougars.

Hosted amid Blenheim's scenic vineyards and fuelled by copious amounts of local produce, MILFest features an array of events designed to appeal to the discerning older woman, including wine tasting, erotic fiction readings and Botox demonstrations. There is also a slew of entertainment targeted at an audience of heavily intoxicated soccer mums, including musical performances from the likes of Sol3 Mio, Opshop and Stan Walker, who are traditionally buried in piles of granny panties thrown from the crowd.

Featuring alongside other such public intoxication classics as Christchurch Cup Week and New Year's at the Mount, MILFest is a staple on the New Zealand social calendar. If you are in the mood to meet masses of middle-aged mothers trying to slough off the tedium of suburban New Zealand with a drunken root, make MILFest your next stop!

Attraction: Pāua House

The height of kitschy Kiwiana, the Pāua House is exactly what it sounds like: a house covered in the discarded shells of over a thousand pāua. The Bluff bungalow was owned by Fred and Myrtle Flutey, who progressively adorned it with pāua shells, ornaments and trinkets over the course of four decades. Obviously, this was in a time when hoarding was viewed as a quirky personality trait rather than a symptom of severe mental illness.

A reported 1 million people visited the Pāua House in Bluff, which is more an indictment on entertainment options in Southland than a recommendation of the iridescent eyesore. The house was an 'iconic' tourist attraction in the same way that the plague was an iconic medieval illness. It was akin to someone in South Auckland decorating their house in nothing but KFC buckets (except that would actually be awesome).

After the Fluteys' deaths, their collection of colourful crap was moved to a replica of their house in the Canterbury Museum, where it remains on display. The Pāua House has proven to be one of the museum's more popular exhibits, along with 'Famous Caucasians of the Canterbury Plains' and 'Custard: Liquid Pākehā'.

Event: Bread & Circus — World Buskers Festival

The preposterously named 'Bread & Circus — World Buskers Festival' is an annual excuse to flood Christchurch with carnies, giving the city a much-needed break from the skinheads that usually clog the streets. The festival consists of 25 relentless days of inescapable 'entertainment' throughout the Garden City's streets, venues and theatres.

Less an artform and more a cry for help, busking usually involves foisting some obscure bullshit on unsuspecting members of the public who are just minding their own business trudging to their dead-end jobs. The World Buskers Festival sees swarms of stilt-walkers, magicians (the worst people in the world) and other clinically depressed losers attempting to entertain vaguely befuddled throngs of Cantabrian locals. It's a great opportunity to see erotic mimes, perverts playing

bagpipes, or recently paroled sex offenders juggling marital aids.

If you suffer from serious psychological issues, you can even sign up to perform at the festival yourself. There's nothing like learning to spin a series of hula hoops while riding a unicycle to take your mind off your dad leaving your mum for your Sunday-school teacher. Bonus dickhead points if you can incorporate a ukulele into your act.

Event: Steampunk NZ Festival

Ōamaru has declared itself the steampunk capital of New Zealand despite having no clear connection to either steam or punks.

For the unfamiliar, steampunk is a retro-futuristic subgenre of science fiction that posits the Victorian age never ended and everybody gets around in zeppelins and has steam-powered butler robots. Quite what this has to do with a penguin-infested shithole in North Otago is entirely unclear, but that hasn't stopped Ōamaruvians from strapping a rocket to a busted old train and calling it a landmark.

The annual Steampunk NZ Festival exists largely as an excuse for IT nerds to engage in group sex — if you've ever dreamed about doing some doggy style while fogging up some goggles or seeing someone get torn apart by a steam-powered fuck machine, then Ōamaru is definitely for you!

Having spectacularly transformed Ōamaru from an economically depressed dump into an economically depressed dump in fancy dress, the success of the festival has inspired the

Coromandel craphole of Thames to create its own similarly shit steampunk event, Steampunk The Thames.

Meanwhile, Ōamaru's capitulation to the steampunk community has resulted in the town being seen as a soft touch for every obscure subculture looking for a hapless hamlet to use as a staging post for their absurd events — within the next year, Ōamaru can look forward to playing host to FurryFest, the Gathering of the Juggalos and the Necrophiliacs' Ball.

Attraction: Moeraki Boulders

Described as an 'unusual' geological phenomenon, the Moeraki Boulders are 'unusual' in the same way your Uncle Neville who smells like coleslaw is 'unusual' — sure there's something a bit different there, but it's probably best if you don't investigate further.

A collection of large spherical stones lying scattered on the beach like empty Speight's cans on the floor of a Dunedin flat after a big night, the Moeraki Boulders are only appealing to people who get their rocks off by looking at actual rocks.

Some people imbue the boulders with mystical powers and claim that if any woman

is to touch one during a full moon while menstruating, they will become instantly pregnant. (Please don't use this excuse while applying for the DPB — WINZ have found rocks notoriously reticent to pay child support.)

Fortunately, it appears that the boulders are gradually eroding in the ceaseless tide, and with any luck will be completely washed away soon, saving scores of helpless travellers from being forced into a dead-boring pitstop.

Attraction: Baldwin Street

Paris has the Champs-Élysées. New Orleans has Bourbon Street. Dunedin has Baldwin Street — a street so terrible at being a street that it has become internationally famous as the steepest example on the planet. The title of World's

Steepest Street is a bit like the title of World's Wettest Desert or World's Tallest Dwarf — it's really only interesting in the sense that it's the best at being the worst.

At the risk of stating the obvious, steepness is not a desirable attribute for a street. When your street has steps in the footpath, can't be tar-sealed and requires a four-wheel drive and balls of steel to drive up, it's clearly too steep. The only reason Baldwin Street is at such an absurd angle is because Dunedin's city grid was laid out by some numpty on the other side of the world who didn't bother to consider the contours of the land, making the whole thing a celebration of colonial-era stupidity.

Popular activities at Baldwin Street include trudging up the punishing slope because you're too chickenshit to drive, taking

'hilarious' photos of the houses on a tilt to make them look crooked, or trying to ride down in a wheelie bin and smashing into a parked car.

Dunedin is so proud of its tenuous claim to fame that when Guinness stripped it of the World's Steepest Street title in 2019 and awarded the title instead to a cobbled lane in a Welsh village, a handful of local nerds staged a protest. One epic pedant even travelled to Wales to measure the new steepest street, pounced on a technicality and harassed Guinness until they reversed the decision — because apparently there's nothing better to do in Dunedin.

All things considered, Baldwin Street tops Dunedin's long list of embarrassing streets — just ahead of Hyde Street, Castle Street and Every Street.

Event: Hyde Street Party

The highlight of Otago University students' social calendar is the annual Hyde Street Party, when hordes of teens take time off from their busy course schedule of furious vaping and complaining about microaggressions to don outlandish costumes and drink themselves into oblivion as they stumble from one mould-riddled hovel of a student flat to the next, leaving behind a trail of drunken destruction. It's basically a pub crawl on steroids, minus the pubs.

Common activities at the Hyde Street Party include alcohol poisoning, low-level sexual assault and egregious abuse of a student loan's 'cost of living' element (which in truth makes it a pretty standard day in Dunedin except it all takes place outside). Emboldened by the fact that it is one of the few Dunedin days when you can actually get your gonads out without them freezing to any flat surface, most revellers get their gonads out, making it a veritable fiesta of fanny and todgers. The ceremonial burning of a couch in the street signifies that partygoers have reached peak drunkenness. The scene could accurately be described as throngs of middle-class white kids doing their best impersonation of a third-world coup.

As a side activity, Hyde Street's student residents compete to decorate their flats according to a theme for the occasion. Popular themes are 'black mould', 'puke-splattered pigsty' and 'drug den', as they require very little preparation.

Note: The Hyde Street Party is not to be confused with the Every Street Party, which features a lot more religious delusions, firearm use and incest.

Event: Bainageddon

Every June, Dunedin is inundated with a throng of fans gathering to celebrate New Zealand's favourite accused mass murderer. Aficionados, known as 'Bainiacs', don their finest ugly sweaters, David Koresh glasses and plastic Prince Charles ears and mark David Bain's acquittal for killing his whole family with a weekend of fun, frivolity and sweater-knitting workshops.

The highlight of the weekend is 'Bain Trail', when the crowd of Bainiacs retrace David's infamous newspaper delivery route, before gathering outside 65 Every Street to participate in a group reading of the famous 111 call. Other activities include a Joe Karam lookalike competition, a target-shooting contest and a Robin Bain memorial caravan makeover demonstration.

80

Athol

Don't be an athol.

Bainageddon has been the subject of a large amount of controversy over the years, but organisers have resisted calls to cancel the event. Some of the strongest criticism has come from David Gray fans, who claim the Aramoana massacre is just as cool.

Bain himself has never attended the event staged in his honour. Desperate to distance himself from the grisly murders, David ditched the sweaters several years ago and legally changed his name to Ashley Bloomfield.

Attraction: Larnach Castle

Looking less like Edinburgh Castle and more like a shit Downton

Abbey, Larnach Castle is billed as 'New Zealand's only castle' — which is only true because the only other things in the country resembling castles are a toy museum in Tīrau and a dairy in Mangatāwhiri.

Castles are emotive buildings promising a riveting history of sieges, depraved aristocrats and bloodthirsty battles. Unfortunately, Larnach Castle features none of that. Instead, it is basically a Victorian version of that property developer who bowls a historic villa and replaces it with a postmodern eyesore.

Larnach Castle was built by Dunedin industrialist and MP William Larnach, who is most famous for lending his name to the 'not-a-castle' and committing suicide at Parliament after finding out his son was having a hoon on his third wife. Due to its owner's untimely demise,

Larnach Castle is reputedly one of the country's most haunted buildings, so is invariably crawling with gronks wanting to be Ghostbusters and other tourists sad enough to believe in that sort of shit.

If you're keen on being charged a fair whack to look at an old house and trudge around an old lady's garden in the depths of an Otago winter, then this place should top your sad little list.

PRESIDENTIAL HIGHWAY

Gore - Clinton 44 km

Memorial highway commemorating America's most prolific exponent of cunnilingus and his climate-change-fighting robot.

TOP 10

REGIONAL STDs

1. Gorenorrhoea (Southland)

2. Chlamyddlemarch (Otago)

3. Hepataihape (Manawatū-Whanganui)

4. Pegasyphilis (Canterbury)

5. Genital Warkworths (Auckland)

6. Bluff Muff (Southland)

7. Dipton Dick (Southland)

8. The Ashburton Gash Squirtin' (Canterbury)

9. Grey Mouth (West Coast)

10. Black Balls (West Coast)

Leaning Tower
of Wanaka
NEW ZEALAND

Puzzling World.

SOUTH ISLAND

WEST COAST ROUTE

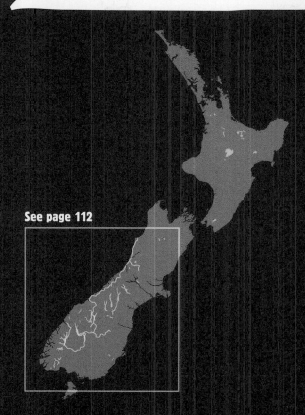

See page 112

Torroland (page 114)

Shantytown Heritage Park (page 115)

Hokitika Driftwood Sign (page 138)
Sock World (page 119)
Wildfoods Festival (page 120)

Arthur's Pass (page 117)

Franz Josef Glacier (page 121)

Cardrona Hotel (page 134)
Cardrona Bra Fence (page 124)

That Wanaka Tree (page 140)
Roys Peak (page 140)
Puzzling World (page 123)

Glenorchy Shed (page 134)

**Milford Sound /
Piopiotahi** (page 129)

Otago Central Rail Trail (page 126)

Giant Takahē

Giant Haemorrhoids

Gondwanalandland
(page 131)

Onsen Hot Pools (page 140)
Queenstown Winter Festival (page 128)

The Giant Blue Chicken, Te Anau.

Attraction: Torroland

A budget 1970s knock-off of Denmark's iconic Lego, Torro joins the long line of disappointing New Zealand 'innovations' that ripped off global icons and produced a shit local version, such as Bata Bullets, the Trekka and *New Zealand Idol*. About as much fun to play with as a fork and a power socket, Torro was only temporarily kept in business by low-decile schools and cheapskate grandmas.

Made in Westport by a company that produced light switches and manufactured from recycled prophylactics, Torro had a semi-soft consistency reminiscent of a baby boomer's unenhanced erection. Sporting a limited range of pieces (aside from a weirdly extensive range of roof bits) and obviously designed by someone who spent most of their time designing light switches, the terrible toy was the height of Kiwi crapness. The stilted creativity afforded by Torro probably goes a long way towards explaining Auckland's ongoing city-planning woes — generations of city planners raised on rubbish Lego can't be expected to figure out where to put trains.

Westport honoured its role as the home of this icon of Kiwi childhood by establishing 'Torroland', a family theme park dedicated to showcasing the awe-inspiring creativity possible with Torro. Visitors can gawk at Torro replicas of such national icons as the Beehive, the Huntly DEKA sign and the Sky Tower (which given the tensile strength of the average Torro brick has developed an unfortunate droop). There is also a scale model of the Pink and White Terraces, but due to Torro's limited colour range it is called the 'Red and Yellow Terraces'. The park even features a selection of fun rides and activities made entirely out of Torro bricks, including a maze, a climbing wall, and a particularly painful slide.

Attraction: Shantytown Heritage Park

A replica of a 19th-century mining town, Shantytown allows visitors to step back in time to an era before electricity, cellphones and women being able to vote, making it only slightly less modern than the rest of the West Coast. As thrilling as the name suggests, Shantytown resembles a ghost town in Scooby-Doo, only without

the fun of being menaced by a property developer dressed as a phantom pirate.

Part-boring museum, part-shit theme park, Shantytown features a collection of old buildings, steam-train rides, and a gold-panning sluice which allows visitors to relive the charm of an era when desperate men stood bollocks-deep in freezing water while doing the 19th-century equivalent of scratching an Instant Kiwi ticket and trying not to contract pneumonia. Children will be thrilled by the prospect of watching a sluice demonstration or trudging from building to building to look at a collection of antiques. It's the type of dryballs destination that mind-numbing school field trips are made of.

There is an additional charge for the privilege of panning for gold — an investment sure to pay off when you become the only person to discover a life-changing amount of gold in a low-rent tourist attraction!

Attraction: Arthur's Pass

Wedged in the heart of the Southern Alps, Arthur's Pass is a scenic passage that crosses the Main Divide and marks the boundary between Canterbury and the West Coast. The pass was named after surveyor Arthur Dudley Dobson, after Dobson learned about it from local Māori and decided to celebrate his ingenuity by naming it after himself, which is basically the geographic equivalent of that bloke who claimed he 'discovered' the clitoris, José Clitoris.

Popular activities in Arthur's Pass include hiking, driving off a viaduct while staring at a waterfall, and getting snowed in during the height of winter and complaining about it on the TV news.

Arthur's Pass is also home to the biggest bird bastard in New Zealand, the kea. Notorious for its 'inquisitive nature', the kea is a dick of a parrot known to nick ciggies, rip rubber from cars and even murder sheep. The so-called 'clowns of the mountain' are about as punishing as actual clowns. Kea are 'cheeky' in the same way that your racist uncle is 'cheeky' — he's actually just a massive prick but everyone is too polite to point it out.

Ironically, the kea now survives on scavenging high-calorie leftovers from visitors, which gives it plenty of energy and ample

free time to focus on relentlessly tormenting those same tourists.

Attraction: Sock World & Sock Knitting Machine Museum

Part sock shop, part vintage sock machine museum and all shit, Hokitika's Sock World claims to be the 'world's greatest sock store', which might be true but it's doubtful that the competition is very stiff. Despite sounding like exactly the sort of thing some mischievous authors might make up to reach the page count for their humour book, Sock World is a real place that actually exists.

Sock World sells a bewildering range of sock-related stock including socks, knitting and sewing supplies (for making socks), gloves (socks for your hands), hats (socks for your head), wank socks, sock machines and sock-machine accessories. One of the most popular displays is the 'History of Love Socks', a chronological tribute to knitted prophylactics.

Despite clearly being a shop masquerading as an educational opportunity, Sock World is one of the most popular attractions in town. Given that the other tourist 'hotspots' in Hokitika are a bunch of driftwood arranged into the name of the town and a prison for the nocturnal national mascot, it's understandable that a museum dedicated to the wonders of knitted footwear has become the top local tourist destination.

If you are the sort of person who is riveted by anachronistic garment manufacture, then Sock World might be the place to blow your proverbial off.

Event: Wildfoods Festival

An annual staple on the West Coast social calendar alongside Blackball's Winter Coalstice and the Great Granity Orgy, Hokitika's Wildfoods Festival celebrates the culinary debauchery of New Zealand's most lawless and toothless region. Founded in 1990, the inaugural festival featured Alison Holst as celebrity judge, who awarded gold to a particularly scrumptious Possum Wellington despite the fact that it contained ingredients that even she wouldn't stuff into a sausage roll.

Attended by all manner of hippies, hillbillies and other undesirables, Wildfoods famously features such out-of-the-box

dishes as huhu grubs, giant snails (aka 'Westcargot') and 'pig nipples on a stick'. Each year, locals attempt to outdo previous winners in the grossness stakes, which has seen the inclusion of such truly stomach-turning delicacies as deep-fried horse testicles, pickled gorse with a drizzle of stallion semen, and even something called 'kale'.

Wildfoods is the only place where you can purchase an actual camel toe or moose knuckle. Interestingly, about the only type of protein not available is human flesh, which is surprising given the dietary inclinations of the average resident of the West Coast.

Hokitika locals celebrate the festival each year by dressing up in ratshit costumes and getting blind drunk, which basically makes Wildfoods the West Coast equivalent of the Wellington Sevens only with less rugby and slightly more inedible food.

Attraction: Franz Josef Glacier

Glaciers are boring. Their name is a synonym for moving so slowly as to be imperceptible. They're basically what would happen if an avalanche decided to have a lie-down. This makes glaciers the ideal attraction for simple-minded folk who are impressed by several million tonnes of frozen water not doing very much not very quickly.

New Zealand's premier glacier is Franz Josef, named after a German pest who never set foot in New Zealand, which makes a change from naming things after English pests who never set foot in New Zealand. Franz Josef is sometimes confused with Tranz Josef, the well-known Auckland drag queen. Because all glaciers

look the same, it is also frequently confused with the nearby Fox Glacier — even the world's top glaciologists don't know which is which.

A big selling point for Franz Josef Glacier is that it is one of the most accessible glaciers in the world, which is a bit like being the most grabbable turd in the toilet — just because you can, doesn't mean you should.

Fortunately, Franz Josef's days as a terrible tourist attraction are numbered. The giant Popsicle is suffering from a case of rapid shrinkage ironically caused by global warming, as opposed to ordinary shrinkage which is caused by colder temperatures. Get disappointed while you still can!

Attraction: Puzzling World

Wānaka's pre-eminent waste of time, Puzzling World is split into two equally disappointing areas: an underwhelming outdoor maze that is more akin to being lost in a garden centre, and an indoor section featuring an array of lacklustre amusements that are less mind-bending than mind-numbing. It's ideal if you want to feel like you are trapped in a ratshit Rubik's Cube or re-create the experience of trying to escape from Josef Fritzl's basement.

Inexplicably, Puzzling World also features an attraction called the 'Roman Toilets', which gives punters the opportunity to take a photo in a replica of a Roman long-drop — the perfect backdrop for some 'Roman cottaging'. The Roman Toilets are literally a shithouse attraction, which is probably why they're free to enter. Warning: Do not take a shit in the Roman Toilets —

the staff get really anal about it.

Puzzling World is packed with slightly befuddled backpackers traipsing from room to room trying to figure out why they wasted perfectly good beer money on this nonsense. Its most impressive illusion is the illusion of good value, while the only puzzle is why anyone would bother spending precious holiday time at such a woeful attraction. Just remember: you can't spell Wānaka without Wanka!

Attraction: Cardrona Bra Fence

Everyone knows there's not enough to look at in the Cardrona Valley, so it's a good thing someone created the Bra Fence. It was the late '90s when a wise head gazed upon some of the most impressive vistas on the planet and thought 'You know what? This is okay but what it really needs is hundreds of bras hung from a wire fence in a haphazard fashion!'

As bras were progressively added to the paddock partition over the years and removed by perverts almost as quickly, the Bra Fence became a major tourist attraction and driver distraction — so much so that the bras had to be moved from the main highway onto a less conspicuous fence alongside a driveway, where the collection now serves as a monument to breast cancer awareness. The origins of the Bra Fence are shrouded in mystery, but speculation suggests it initially started as a means for a local

serial killer to display trophies of his kills.

The Bra Fence is a source of considerable controversy among residents of the Cardrona Valley, with some regarding it as an eyesore and a traffic hazard, while others think it is awesome because bras touch titties and titties are awesome. Visitors should be aware that despite the presence of an almost incalculable number of bras, the chances you will see an actual boob remain exceptionally slim.

Despite critics claiming the Bra Fence is a tourist booby trap that milks its popularity, you'll feel like a real tit if you let the knockers put you off. Don't get sucked into the tit-for-tat between the local boobs and the udder side. If you're in the general areola, nip down for a look. Some say it's the breast attraction in Central Otago — even better than the Breast Hill Track or Mount Tititea. It's certainly a place that will live on in your mammaries forever.

Did you know? The Bra Fence has a sister attraction in Milan's Panty Fountain that fires out women's sodden undergarments on an hourly basis.

Attraction: Otago Central Rail Trail

Formerly a train line between Middlemarch and Clyde, the Otago Central Rail Trail is now a 150-kilometre makeshift cycleway, affording anyone the opportunity to live out their fantasy of being a train.

A two-wheeled tour of some of Central Otago's premier shit towns, the trail passes through the sort of settlements where 'quaint' is a euphemism for 'lack of running water'. Local residents pride themselves on

their 'Southern hospitality', which is exactly as much a scene from *Deliverance* as it sounds like. 'Southern hospitality' is officially defined as when hoteliers stop talking shit about Aucklanders for long enough to take their money.

Long, boring and riddled with South Islanders, the Otago Central Rail Trail is an ideal holiday for the sort of exceedingly dull bastards who are unable to resist the prospect of sitting all day on a rock-hard bike seat designed by sadists to inflict as much genital pain as possible, all so they can gaze upon stunning vistas of sheep paddocks, cow paddocks and the occasional horse paddock for variety.

The entire trail is furnished in gravel for maximum discomfort, inefficiency and injury potential, and garnished with numerous small mountains of horse shit. Despite this, on any given day it is filled with a phalanx of obese boomers drizzled into Lycra gimp suits and perched precariously on creaking ebikes — the type of scenery purposely not mentioned in the brochures.

Picking a good time to tackle the trail is difficult — in summer Otago is blisteringly hot, while in winter it's frozen and frigid. The shit town of Alexandra, on the trail, is both the hottest and the coldest in the country. On balance, the best time to do it is never.

Event: Queenstown Winter Festival

Each year, more than 45,000 people swarm into Queenstown to mark the opening of the ski fields at the overcrowded and overpriced mountain town's Winter Festival. Ostensibly celebrating the Ringo of seasons in New Zealand's capital of frigid pretension, the Queenstown Winter Festival is actually an elaborate scam to engage in some council-events-funding-facilitated midwinter bonking with intoxicated strangers. There's nothing like getting your bollocks snap-frozen to a stainless-steel handrail while engaging in a spot of dogging in front of a picture-postcard backdrop.

The Winter Festival claims to feature events such as downhill skiing, snowboarding and snowtubing, none of which are actual sports but rather codewords for various sexual shenanigans engaged in by mountainfolk. If you meet someone who claims to be into cross-country skiing, they are actually inviting you to an orgy.

The Queenstown Winter Festival isn't just dominated by shagging or careening down a mountain on various implements — it also features an array of mind-numbing 'iconic' events such as Dog Derby, Hospo Race and a Birdman Festival where locals attempt to bring a quick end to it all by jumping into a freezing lake. The festival also sports an execrable lineup of 'entertainers' that in the past has included such luminaries as decrepit Aussie rocker Jimmy Barnes, decrepit Kiwi rocker Dave Dobbyn and even something called 'The Feelers', which sounds like a support group for child molesters.

Attraction: Milford Sound / Piopiotahi

Milford Sound is named after a harbour in Wales that some guy went to some time. Aside from being entirely unimaginative, the English name is perhaps one of the most blatant cases of false advertising ever committed — it is neither a sound (rather a fiord), and nor is it home to a bevy of attractive older women (there are zero MILFs on offer). The original Māori name, Piopiotahi, is a wonderfully evocative word referencing a poetic tale of loss and grief, so anyone who uses it rather than the boring English alternative will send any talkback-listening boomer into a fit of apoplexy.

Situated in Fiordland (which sounds like a particularly boring Scandinavian theme park), Milford Sound sports the sort of excessive natural beauty that is almost stomach-churning — it's a little bit like a professional model who complains about 'getting fat' after eating half a sandwich so you are forced to tell her how

skinny she looks in those jeans. Indeed, the wild and remote landscape is so awe-inspiring that it will force you to gaze into the inky black water, admit that the only thing blacker than the sea is your soul, and finally confront the fact that you are a complete waste of meat and spunk.

The picturesque vistas of Milford Sound, however, come at a price. The fiord is not the most accessible, being a couple of hours from a proper town and over three hours from a proper airport. Over a million visitors make the punishing pilgrimage each year, so you will invariably be crammed arsehole-to-ankles with a bevy of German hikers and gormless American travel bloggers trying to tick another 'must-do' off their *Lonely Planet* checklist.

Milford Sound is also one of the wettest places on Earth — topped only by your aunty's knickers after a Michael Bolton concert — so is great fun if you enjoy taking cold showers with your clothes on. It is home to two permanent waterfalls, which are fantastic if you ever wondered what happens when water meets gravity.

Attraction: Gondwanalandland

New Zealand has some legendary extinct creatures: the mighty moa, the giant Haast's eagle, the non-inbred South Islander. These and other examples of native primeval flora and fauna are celebrated at the Southland theme park Gondwanalandland.

The park's star attraction is a flock of live moa, a defective species of flightless bird that the Almighty decided to wipe from the face of the Earth for the crime of basically being an ostrich with

a bad attitude. Thanks to cutting-edge 1990s technology, scientists were able to resurrect the beast using a drop of moa semen extracted from the fossilised remains of a gay mosquito. They then whipped up a second batch after the first colony was killed by a misplaced drop of 1080. Unfortunately, sequence gaps in the salvaged moa DNA forced scientists to supplement it with genetic material from a pūkeko, causing the moa to turn out blue.

Located on a remote island in Fiordland and accessible only by helicopter, Gondwanalandland was created by eccentric businessman and native bird enthusiast Gareth Morgan in 1993. Morgan was fascinated by the prospect of reviving an extinct species and also by the idea of birds big enough to kill cats. Unfortunately for Morgan and park visitors alike, moa are actually herbivores, so they mostly stand around eating shrubs and behaving like big chickens rather than doing anything actually interesting.

Gondwanalandland also houses tuatara, the lizard-looking things that you can only see at any other tourist attraction in the country. Ōtorohanga Kiwi House & Native Bird Park has them. Kelly Tarlton's Sea Life Aquarium has them. Hell, Hokitika Sock World probably has them. It seems there isn't a theme that you can't crowbar a tuatara into. Despite their rather fearsome visage, tuatara are even less entertaining than moa, spending their entire lives standing perfectly still like those losers who paint themselves silver and loiter in public places pretending to be statues. They could replace the tuatara with toys and no one would know the difference.

In recent years, possibly due to the fact that most of the inmates are as dull as a day in Greymouth, Gondwanalandland has fallen into a state of disrepair. In an effort to revive the popularity of the park, science dorks brought back the moa's only natural predator, the Haast's eagle — an unfortunate development that saw several toddlers picked up and dropped from a great height. There have also been instances of small children and midgets being trampled by moa. Despite the numerous deaths at Gondwanalandland, the park inexplicably keeps reopening after each massacre with a selection of even more dangerous species, until basically the same plot inevitably unfolds again.

TOP 20
MOST OVERRATED PHOTO OPS

1. **Cardrona Hotel**
   It's just a decrepit building that looks like an old shed.

2. **Glenorchy Shed**
   It's just an old shed.

3. **Bra Fence (Cardrona)**
   Normally, taking photos of women's underwear would get you locked up.

4. **Hundertwasser Toilets (Kawakawa)**
   Normally, taking photos of a public loo would get you locked up.

5. **Giant L&P Bottle (Paeroa)**
   A corporate advertisement commonly mistaken for a tourist attraction.

6. **Kent Road (Taranaki)**
   Blessed with the backdrop of a perfectly aligned Mount Taranaki, Kent Road is an irresistible photo spot for numerous nitwits who think that plonking themselves in the middle of a 100 km/h highway makes them look cool.

1.

2.

6.

7. **Infinity Pools (Anawhata Beach)**
Located on clearly marked private property, these clifftop waterfall pools are a popular spot for intrepid trespassers to photograph themselves swimming, pissing or fucking in the local residents' water supply.

8. **Aeroplane McDonald's (Taupō)**
This fast-food joint partly housed in an old aeroplane proudly proclaims itself the 'World's Coolest McDonald's', but looks more like the aftermath of an Al-Qaeda attack.

9. **Mud pools (Rotorua)**
Come to New Zealand and let steam fuck up your camera lens while you risk third-degree burns to get a photo of some hot mud!

10. **Mount Maunganui summit (Tauranga)**
Because we haven't already seen enough photos of that exact view.

11. **Blue Spring (Putaruru)**
Once a semi-secret swimming spot, social media made the Blue Spring so popular that pollution from bathers left it in danger of becoming the Brown Spring. While you're no longer allowed to dip your disgusting bits in the freezing water, you can still get your car broken into while taking a selfie in front of the weedy waterway.

7.

8.

9.

10.

11.

12. Direction Signs (Cape Rēinga and Bluff)

The famous yellow multi-pronged signposts at either end of the country point to every location they can think of — a not-so-subtle hint to leave immediately. The arse-end version at Bluff gets bonus shit points for being wildly inaccurate.

13. Mosgiel Sign

A cringeworthy copy of the Hollywood sign which only serves to remind everyone how dull and pointless Mosgiel is.

14. Hokitika Driftwood Sign

A tangle of twigs contorted into the word 'Hokitika', which no one has gotten around to clearing away.

15. DEKA Sign (Huntly)

The last remnant of a defunct department store chain that went out of business sometime when the current prime minister was in primary school, Huntly's derelict DEKA sign is only popular among celebrators of shitness.

16. Lake Tekapo

Famous for its weird sky-blue hue, Lake Tekapo looks like it's filled with something gross and toxic like Toilet Duck or Gatorade.

2.

14.

15.

3.

16.

17. That Wanaka Tree

Girt by lake and framed by Alps, 'That Wanaka Tree' might be the most photographed plant in the country. Not even the recent castration of its lower branch could dampen the insatiable demand for selfies with the sickly old shrub.

18. Giant Sheep and Dog (Tīrau)

A selfie with the supersized corrugated-iron sheep or dog is a surefire way to confuse the shit out of your friends and family back home.

19. Onsen Hot Pools (Queenstown)

Re-enact a cliche by getting someone to take a photo of your back while you stew in a big barrel of hot water. Bonus points if you're flashing your norks at a mountain.

20. Roys Peak (Wānaka)

What the carefully cropped Instagram/Tinder/Grindr pics don't show is the huge line of lemmings queuing for their turn to pose, having just slogged up a mountain for half a day for the privilege.

7.

8.

8.

19.

20.

TOP 5
RACIST STATUES

New Zealand is a smorgasbord for fans of racist statues — all Kiwi cities and many small towns are littered with bronze bigots, marble murderers and other busts of bastards. The following five are just the tip of the shitberg.

1. **Captain James Cook**
   Who: He wasn't the first person to arrive in Aotearoa. He wasn't even the first honky. But he was the first Pom, paving the way for the country's colonisation and the subjugation of the resident Māori population.
   Location: Numerous sites across the country, most controversially in the Gisborne area, where Cook first landed in Aotearoa before his crew murdered and raped a handful of locals. Gizzy hosts a pair of Captain Cooks — including one inexplicably dressed in Italian naval garb.
   Racism rating: ★★★★★

2. **Sir George Grey**
   Who: Former New Zealand premier and governor, responsible for the Waikato Wars and the theft of massive amounts of Māori land. He later did some awesome colonialism in that hotbed

Captain Cook, Gisborne.

of racial harmony South Africa, before retiring to Kawau Island to fondle some wallabies.

Location: Albert Park, Auckland.
Racism rating: ★★★★★

3. Colonel Marmaduke Nixon

Who: Despite having a name reminiscent of a cartoon dog, Marmaduke Nixon was a very real person who led a very real minor massacre of civilians at unfortified Rangiaowhia in 1864 (the massacre was only minor in that most of its victims were minors). His bravery in the face of unarmed children and the elderly is memorialised with a roadside monument.
Location: Ōtāhuhu, Auckland.
Racism rating: ★★★★★

4. Captain John Hamilton

Who: Another British commander in the New Zealand Wars, tasked with killing Māori and stealing their land. Hamilton was punished by having the country's STD capital named after him.
Location: Originally in Hamilton's Civic Square, the statue was removed in 2020 at the request of Waikato-Tainui.
Racism rating: ★★★★

5. Colin Meads

Who: Rugby player and deer velvet enthusiast who toured apartheid South Africa as part of an all-white All Blacks team in 1960, before defying a boycott to coach the NZ Cavaliers on their unauthorised tour of the racist state in 1986.
Location: Te Kūiti town centre.
Racism rating: ★★★

TOP 10

ADVENTURE ACTIVITIES

1. **Tramping (Tasman, Fiordland, Tongariro)**
   Get lost wandering in dense bush, and trigger a search and rescue operation costing hundreds of thousands of dollars.

2. **Snowboarding (Queenstown, Mount Hutt, Ruapehu)**
   Hurtle down a mountain on a flimsy sheet of fibreglass.

3. **Skiing (Queenstown, Mount Hutt, Ruapehu)**
   Hurtle down a mountain on two flimsy sheets of fibreglass.

4. **Jet boating (Queenstown, West Coast, Rotorua)**
   Careen down a rapid-filled river at high speed until you collide with a rock.

5. **Whale watching (Kaikōura, Bay of Islands, Bay of Plenty)**
   Cram into an unseaworthy vessel alongside some suspiciously sweaty Japanese tourists to watch the obese shut-ins of the ocean loll about like the long-term unemployed on benefit day.

6. Whitewater rafting (Queenstown, West Coast, Rotorua)

Careen down a rapid-filled river at low speed until you collide with a rock.

7. Bungy jumping (Queenstown, Taupō, Auckland)

Confront the spectre of death by leaping off a bridge, platform or tower with a giant rubber band tied around your ankles.

8. Skydiving (Queenstown, Taupō)

Confront the spectre of death by leaping out of a plane with nothing tied to your ankles, you absolute fucking maniac.

9. Skyline Gondola & Luge (Queenstown, Rotorua)

Get tugged up a hill in a glass box before rolling down again on a plastic cart that goes just fast enough to make crashing into a tree a reasonable possibility, but not quite fast enough to actually be fun. Despite the name, there are no canal boats or toboggans.

10. Zorbing (Rotorua)

Bounce down a hill in a vomit-filled bubble until you pass out.

TOP 10

ACTIVITIES FOR BORING CUNTS

1. Look at a sheep.

2. Touch a rock.

3. Stare at a tree.

4. Eat some plain white toast.

5. Go to a museum.

6. Take a walking tour.

7. Go to an art gallery.

8. Read a book.

9. Sit quietly and wait for your holiday to end.

10. Do a *Lord of the Rings* tour.

HORSE
POO
SMALL $5
LARGE $10

FREE DELIVERY
4 LARGE BAGS
ute Loads
available

Tip: Make time to stop in small towns to try the local delicacies.

TOP 10
PLACES TO EAT

1. Bugger Café (Pipiroa)

New Zealand's top-rated sodomy-themed roadside pitstop. Perfect for a lonely trucker a long way from home.

2. Cake the Muss (South Auckland)

Inspired by an iconic character from *Once Were Warriors*, this café is a great option if you want a burly man to cook you some fucking eggs or serve you up a knuckle sandwich.

3. Mussolini's (Dipton)

Known for its authentic Italian fare such as lasagne toppers, tinned spaghetti on toast, and pizzas with plenty of pineapple.

4. Lummis Hummus (Wellington)

Named after inaugural *New Zealand Idol* winner Ben Lummis, this Cuba Street takeaway does a great falafel — and you can even meet Ben himself if you visit during his shift.

5. Yellow-Fried Penguin (Ōamaru)
Arguably North Otago's hottest takeaway joint, 'YFP' reputedly serves the world's best battered rockhopper.

6. Planet Shorty Street (Auckland)
A themed restaurant owned by *Shortland Street* actors Michael Galvin, Karl Burnett and John Leigh. Think Planet Hollywood but much, much, much worse.

7. The Cleft Palate (Gore)
This popular Southern pub is run by husband-and-wife-and-brother-and-sister duo Fred and Frida Fennimore-Fennimore. The only beer on tap is Speights and the only food is cheese rolls (i.e. cheese inbred), which are rolled onsite by the eleven Fennimore-Fennimore children's own 23 hands.

8. Moister Than An Oyster (Bluff)
New Zealand's only combined brothel/seafood restaurant. We recommend the fresh Bluff oysters and Staci.

9. State Highway Yum (Tirau)
The most appropriate eatery for a road trip, this SH1 café offers a menu consisting entirely of highway roadkill. The pūkeko pie is popular, while the pan-fried possum testicles are a treat.

10. Ku Klux Khicken (Christchurch)
Specialises in white meats.

TOP 10
PLACES TO STAY

1. **Hooker Lodge (Taupō)**
   Nestled in an idyllic riverside setting with unparalleled privacy, Hooker Lodge offers luxury boutique accommodation for the discerning gentleman and his nocturnal companion. It is actually the world's most expensive hotel that charges by the hour.

2. **Hang Out Hostel (Queenstown)**
   For a unique experience, try this hip new hostel where you can snooze in a sleeping bag as it dangles from a bridge by a bungy cord.

3. **Gloriahole (Haupiri)**
   Cut off from the hustle and bustle of the outside world, this self-sufficient Christian commune is a great place to stay if you're a vulnerable person looking to be exploited. The price is steep (all your money and everything you own) but as long as you work hard and don't be female, you'll have a blast.

4. **Hotel Torroland (Westport)**
   Situated at Westport's Torroland amusement park and made entirely from New Zealand's shit Lego knock-off Torro, this hotel is a family-

friendly option — although the floor does hurt like hell to walk on.

5. A Toyota Corolla (Ōtara)

With Auckland's skyrocketing property and rental prices beyond many people's reach, living in a car is so in right now. Get the authentic South Auckland experience by staying in this well-presented 2001 five-door in Ōtara.

6. Fennimore's B&B (Gore)

Fred and Frida Fennimore-Fennimore of The Cleft Palate fame also run this charming B&B with their extensive brood. Guests are treated to nightly banjo performances by Fred 'Fingers' Fennimore-Fennimore himself, before being strongly encouraged to partake in a variety of late-night games with Fingers and his friends.

7. New Zealand's Smallest Hotel (Wellington)

While some might confuse New Zealand's Smallest Hotel with a wheelie bin, the truly discerning will appreciate the minimalist experience — if folding yourself in half to fit inside isn't your bag, then you can at least take the opportunity to pretend to be Oscar the Grouch.

8. Vaivara Grove (Whitianga)

Run by some authentically smelly hippies, this organic commune provides guests with a ready supply of curdled beans and a spot to sleep in a communal yurt in return for hours of backbreaking labour. Why take a holiday when you can cosplay slavery?

9. Auckland Prison (Pāremoremo)

The comfort level and strict rules at this basic accommodation provider might leave something to be desired, but you can't beat the price. Note: There is a minimum stay.

10. Anywhere you want (anywhere you want)

If there's one type of tourist Kiwis love, it's a freedom camper. Anywhere will do: designated areas, places where freedom camping is explicitly banned, public parks, people's front lawns — simply pitch your $20 tent or park up your people-mover packed with filthy backpackers and you're good to go! Don't forget to shit all over the ground before you depart your favoured spot.

INDEX